T0195705

EVERYBODY HAS TO GO

Simple Reminders That Life Happens to All of Us

DIONNE BELL

WESTBOW
P R E S S®
A DIVISION OF THOMAS NELSON
& ZONDERVAN

WestBow Press books may be ordered through
booksellers or by contacting:

WestBow Press
A Division of Thomas Nelson & Zondervan
1663 Liberty Drive
Bloomington, IN 47403
www.westbowpress.com
1 (866) 928-1240

Scripture quotations taken from The Holy Bible, New International
Version® NIV® Copyright © 1973 1978 1984 2011 by Biblica,
Inc. TM. Used by permission. All rights reserved worldwide.

ISBN: 978-1-9736-8887-7 (sc)
ISBN: 978-1-9736-8886-0 (e)

Library of Congress Control Number: 2020905283

Print information available on the last page.

WestBow Press rev. date: 3/19/2020

To Christopher, Kayla, and Kristin

What has been will be again, what was done will be done again; there is nothing new under the sun.

—Ecclesiastes 1:9

INTRODUCTION

This is a collection of simple reminders that whatever you encounter, you can endure. Others have, and so too will you.

1

EVERYBODY HAS TO GO.

Don't be easily embarrassed, especially by things that are common to all healthy human beings.

Don't fret too much. We all trip, fall, pass gas, and go number 2.

2

IT IS NOT ALWAYS ABOUT
YOU. IN FACT, IT IS
RARELY ABOUT YOU.

3

EVERYONE HAS A BAD DAY.

The cashier. The teacher. The customer service representative. The pastor. The doctor. The bank teller. The radio host. The airplane pilot. The police officer. Men and women of every profession have bad days.

When someone is rougher, ruder, sassier, and snippier than you believe necessary, keep in mind that they—like you at times—may simply be having a bad day.

Hint: refer to number 2.

4

ALL YOU HAVE IS NOW.

Worrying about yesterday is an utter waste of time. Since you can't change the past, it is depressing to worry about it.

Worrying about tomorrow is also an exercise in futility since the next day, hour, and minute are not guaranteed.

Embrace the current moment and experience it to the fullest.

5

FEW THINGS MAKE LIFE BETTER THAN LAUGHTER.

A healthy sense of humor is the brush that paints every circumstance a brighter hue.

Laugh. A lot.

6

ONE THING MORE VITAL THAN LAUGHTER IS GRATITUDE.

Gratitude is the prescription to cure all manner of diseases, including entitlement, selfishness, and greed, to name a few.

7

MORE IMPORTANT THAN LAUGHTER, GRATITUDE, AND EVERYTHING ELSE IS LOVE.

Love is patient, love is kind. It does not envy, it does not boast, it is not proud.

It does not dishonor others, it is not self-seeking, it is not easily angered, it keeps no record of wrongs.

Love does not delight in evil but rejoices with the truth.

It always protects, always trusts, always hopes, always perseveres. Love never fails. (1 Corinthians 13:4–8)

8

NEVER COMPARE YOURSELF TO OTHERS.

You.

Are.

Enough.

Period!

The world has benefited from having one Abraham Lincoln. One Gandhi. One Albert Einstein. One Martin, one Malcom, and one Mandela. One Sammy, Sinatra, Smokey, Elvis, Wonder, and Mr. Wonderful. One Oprah. One Ellen. One Poe, Shakespeare, Maya, and King–Stephen, that is. One Jackson, Jordan, and Tyson.

The best you can offer this world is the one and only *you!*

Comparing "up" makes you feel less than and inferior.

Comparing "down" makes you feel greater than and superior.

Neither is correct or true.

9

DON'T ENVY WHAT OTHER PEOPLE HAVE.

What is meant for another person may not be meant for you. Don't begrudge anyone anything.

Get a plan. Get to praying. Get to work.

10

YOU MAY FAIL, BUT YOU ARE NOT A FAILURE.

Failure is a fee we pay to travel the road of success.

As long as you continue driving, you can never be a failure.

11

THE TRULY STRONG RECOGNIZE THEIR OWN WEAKNESSES.

Don't be quicker to recognize and point out others' weaknesses and faults than you are to recognize your own.

Self-improvement will keep you too busy to dedicate time trying to fix other people.

> Why do you look at the speck of sawdust in your brother's eye and pay no attention to the plank in your own eye?
>
> How can you say to your brother, "Let me take the speck out of your eye,"

when all the time there is a plank in your own eye?

You hypocrite, first take the plank out of your own eye, and then you will see clearly to remove the speck from your brother's eye. (Matthew 7:3–5)

12

NINE TIMES OUT OF TEN, THE BULLY WAS BULLIED.

The phrase "hurting people hurt people" is true.

People often perpetuate treatment they've received.

The bully lacks confidence, security, and strength.

You'd do better to encounter the bully with prayer and compassion than with fear.

Hint: refer to number 2.

*Always report bullying that you witness or experience.

13

EACH PERSON HAS TO WANT IT FOR HIM- OR HERSELF.

No matter how much you love people, you can't force them to change their mind-set or behavior—even if it *is* for the better.

Remember: you can't want for others more than they want for themselves. Maybe they are not willing or physically or emotionally ready to change.

Fret not. If and when they come around is not a reflection on you.

Try not to drive yourself nuts over other people being complacent about their situations.

Hint: you got it—number 2.

14

WHAT IS INSIDE
ALWAYS COMES OUT.

The way people treat you has more do to with who *they* are than with who *you* are.

The mouth and hands directly reflect the heart and mind. In other words, what is on the outside (how people talk and behave) reveals what comprises the inside.

> No good tree bears bad fruit, nor does a bad tree bear good fruit. Each tree is recognized by its own fruit. People do not pick figs from thorn bushes, or grapes from briers.
>
> A good man brings good things out of the good stored up in his heart, and

an evil man brings evil things out of the evil stored up in his heart. For the mouth speaks what the heart is full of. (Luke 6:43–45)

15

NOBODY OWES
YOU ANYTHING.

Despite how marvelous, wonderful, and special as your parent(s) may have told you you were, life will show you otherwise.

The world will in fact not revolve around you.

You will experience fewer disappointments if you view opportunities and good fortune as gifts of grace rather than expected entitlements.

16

FAIR IS A PLACE WITH RIDES, COTTON CANDY, AND PEANUTS. PERIOD.

Sorry to say it, but life just isn't fair.

Cheaters oftentimes win.

Good guys do finish last.

Sometimes, really bad things happen to really good people.

Educators are underpaid.

Nurses are overworked.

Manners are as antique as cursive writing.

Men can eat a dozen donuts and not gain an ounce, while women gain twenty pounds just looking at the box.

We gotta take the good with the bad.

> When times are good, be happy; but when times are bad, consider this: God has made the one as well as the other. Therefore, no one can discover anything about their future. (Ecclesiastes 7:14)

17

GIVE MORE THAN YOU TAKE.

Giving in greater proportion than taking keeps the world balanced.

18

COMPLAINING IS AN EXERCISE IN FUTILITY.

Nobody enjoys the company of a complainer.

Chronic complainers, weighed down by the weight of their discontent and ingratitude, transfer their burdens to those unfortunate enough to suffer their lament.

Venting and expression are perfectly healthy, natural, and productive.

Conversely, complaining is about as effective as trying to run from New York to California—on a treadmill! A lot of time and energy are exerted on a road going nowhere.

19

FORGIVENESS IS VITAL.

Just as detergent removes stains from clothing, so does forgiveness remove poison from your mind, body, and soul.

Bitterness and unforgiveness are noxious. When you hold onto them, you erode from the inside out.

Unforgiveness is a self-inflicted insult on top of the injury another person levied against you.

Never add insult to injury!

Forgiveness doesn't mean a person's actions should be excused. Forgiveness means your *need* to move on from a hurtful person or situation outweighs your *desire* for revenge.

Forgiveness is never about the person who wronged you; it actually has nothing to do with him or her. When it comes to forgiveness, it is *always* about you.

> The weak can never forgive. Forgiveness is an attribute of the strong. (Mahatma Gandhi)

20

YOUR ATTITUDE COLORS ALL OF YOUR LIFE EXPERIENCES.

Just because situations and circumstances are negative doesn't mean your disposition has to be. You aren't usually joyful *because of* the storm, but you can be joyful *despite* the storm. And you can exude grace *through* the storm.

There is no rainbow without rain.

There is no testimony without a test.

There is no warrior without a war.

A positive attitude will take you farther than degrees, talent, money, physical appearance, popularity, or anything else.

21

IN ALL YOU DO, ACT AS THOUGH SOMEONE IS WATCHING AND LISTENING—BECAUSE SOMEONE IS.

No matter who you are, where you are, or what you do, you are setting an example for at least one other person.

Act accordingly.

22

BE CONFIDENT,
NEVER ARROGANT.

Confident people are sincere and secure; this enables them to uplift others.

Arrogant people put others down.

Arrogance is the mask that hides the wearer's insecurities, inadequacies, and fears.

23

BE MINDFUL OF THE COLOR OF YOUR LICENSE PLATE.

In my home state, those with DUI/OVI convictions have license plates that are bright yellow and red.

Instead of gaping at the driver, aghast at his or her misbehavior, we should consider what color our license plate would be if our worst habit, decision, or weakness were displayed.

How many brightly hued, accusatory license plates would dot the roads if we were convicted of lying, gossip, adultery, pride, gluttony, perfectionism, judgmentalism, bullying, abusive behavior, or cheating on tests, taxes, or term papers?

> Stop judging by mere appearances, but
> instead judge correctly. (John 7:24)

24

WRITE THIRTEEN POSITIVE ATTRIBUTES OR CHARACTERISTICS ABOUT YOURSELF.

Have you ever realized how difficult it is to believe and accept compliments? It is even harder to name our positive attributes. We all have goodness in us. Being secure with that fact enables us to recognize goodness in others.

Being able to sit comfortably with yourself will allow you to walk confidently with others.

25

NOBODY CAN PLEASE EVERYBODY.

Always be kind, even to the unkind.

Always be courteous, even to the rude.

You will never make all people happy all the time.

Trying to do so will stress, depress, and mess with you.

You will end up emotionally fatigued, while the very people you're trying to please will remain unsatisfied, entitled, and ever demanding.

26

DON'T OFFER UNSOLICITED ADVICE: I KNOW IT MAY BE DIFFICULT AT TIMES, BUT YOU MUST LEARN TO BITE YOUR TONGUE.

People rarely apply *solicited* advice, so do others as well as yourself a favor: save your time and breath by not offering *unsolicited* advice.

The expectant mother really does not appreciate hearing about your first trimester sickness or third trimester swollen ankles.

Allow the new employee in your department to form his or her own opinions about who is never to be trusted.

Spewing unsolicited advice wearies the listener, and it makes you seem like a know-it-all.

27

EVERYBODY HAS A RELATIVE HE OR SHE WOULD TRADE FOR A WOODEN NICKEL.

Moochers. Drug Addicts. Liars. Fighters. Thieves. Braggarts. Airheads. Compulsive gamblers. Chronic complainers. Sanctimonious hypocrites. Gossips. Bullies. Perfectionists. Perpetual victims ...

We all have 'em in our families, so don't be embarrassed by the ones in yours.

Test: right now, I bet you can picture the family member who comes to every family event empty-handed yet leaves with enough food to feed a small country!

Take heart. You're not alone.

28

MATERIAL POSSESSIONS DO NOT GUARANTEE LASTING HAPPINESS.

The only 100 percent guarantee the continual acquisition of material things provides is that you will have a lot of *stuff.*

Stuff can, and actually will at some point, be lost or stolen, deteriorate, or be left for people to fight over ten minutes after you die.

> Then He said to them, "watch out! Be on your guard against all kinds of greed; life does not consist in an abundance of possessions." (Luke 12:15)

29

TRY TO ENGAGE IN AT *LEAST* ONE FIGHT EVERY DAY.

Be intentionally determined to lay it all on the line in battle daily.

Some things you may fight for include the following:

- your marriage
- your healthier/cleaner living
- your financial freedom
- your family
- your friendships
- your sobriety
- your peace of mind
- your new business venture or creative idea

30

EVERYBODY NEEDS SOMEONE WHO BELIEVES IN HIM OR HER. BE SOMEONE'S CHEERLEADER.

People tend to ascend, or descend, to the expectations that others have of them.

When you see potential in people, tell them. Then provide them the resources and opportunities to meet the stated expectation.

They will blow it out of the water!

Nothing boosts confidence in someone like your expressed belief in him or her.

The other side of that coin is this: don't punish people or hold them accountable for not meeting expectations that are not communicated. Most people aren't mind readers.

31

EVERYONE CAN LEARN SOMETHING FROM ANYONE.

Embrace the idea that not only do you *not* know everything, but every person you encounter can teach you something.

Even a broken clock is right twice a day!

32

WE ALL NEED ONE TRUE FRIEND.

Two are better than one, because they have a good return for their labor:

If either of them falls down, one can help the other up. But pity anyone who falls and has no one to help them up.

Also, if two lie down together, they will keep warm. But how can one keep warm alone?

Though one may be overpowered, two can defend themselves. A cord of three strands is not quickly broken. (Ecclesiastes 4:9–12)

33

EVERYONE WANTS TO BE HEARD.

All people have a voice. Acknowledging another person's voice affirms he or she is not invisible.

When you observe people talking terribly, behaving badly, and acting atrociously, it is often an attempt to be heard by any means necessary.

34

ALL OF US MAKE MISTAKES.

Nobody is perfect. Lighten up on yourself, and others.

35

EVERYBODY HAS HAD A FIRST DAY.

Everybody has had a first day

- on the job
- at school
- as a parent
- driving
- cooking

Whatever it is, nobody was born doing it.

Be patient and empathetic with people (including yourself) during the learning process. We are all works in progress—at least we *should* be.

36

EMBRACE DIVERSITY. NO TWO PEOPLE ARE THE SAME.

Even those who share the same DNA have different likes and dislikes, personality traits, and emotions.

Everyone is not like you; that is fine.

People will not express joy, pain, excitement, grief, anger, or love the way you do.

And that's okay!

Uniformity is dull.

> Always remember that you are absolutely unique. Just like everyone else. (Margaret Mead)

37

EACH PERSON HAS A STORY.

No one person has a monopoly on pain, abuse, struggle and adversity, trials and tribulations, or disappointments.

Don't use your troubled past or horrible experiences to excuse your inappropriate behavior and bad choices.

Intentionally use your storied past to create brighter tomorrows.

As you encourage, empower, and embolden yourself, you will also (possibly unknowingly) inspire others to do likewise.

38

DO NOT ALLOW YOURSELF TO GET SUCKED IN.

There are times when people will intentionally push your buttons. The aphorism "Misery loves company" is true.

Avoid the trap of someone else's catastrophe.

Decline the invitation to someone else's debacle.

Instead of being sucked in, you may walk away, take a deep breath, count to ten, or say sandpaper five times quietly to yourself. Compare the aggressive person to a piece of sandpaper; rough, harsh and abrasive. The more they grind and rub you the wrong way, the more ragged, tattered, and torn they become. The more you resist, the more polished, poised, and perfected you become.

My dear brothers and sisters, take note of this: Everyone should be quick to listen, slow to speak and slow to become angry, because human anger does not produce the righteousness that God desires. (James 1:19)

39

CHOOSE CHARACTER OVER REPUTATION TEN OUT OF TEN TIMES.

Your reputation is what others believe about you despite what is true.

Your character is what is true of you despite what others believe.

40

DON'T BEGRUDGE OTHERS' GOOD FORTUNE.

The blessings with which God clothes someone else will not likely fit you. Take comfort knowing that God is always tenderly loving, in complete control, astutely aware, and infinitely capable. What he has for you is for you, and what is for others is for them. In fact, be genuinely joyful when others around you are being blessed. It is a reminder of how close your blessing is!

41

MIND THE COMPANY YOU KEEP.

Walk with the wise and become wise, for a companion of fools suffers harm. (Proverbs 13:20)

42

DO YOUR OWN HOMEWORK.

Because something *is* in the history books doesn't mean it happened as written. Do you really beleieve that Christohper Columbus, or Amerigo Vespucci, sailed the ocean blue?

Because something *isn't* is the history books (e.g., the Greenwood Massacre in Tulsa, Oklahoma) doesn't mean it did *not* happen.

Look for the truth behind a thing.

Reading it in a book, magazine, or online does not make it true.

43

READ. A LOT. THEN READ SOME MORE!

Reading stretches and benefits the mind and imagination in the same way yoga does the body.

Reading is the quickest, easiest, and cheapest way to travel worlds and galaxies, meeting all kinds of interesting characters along the way.

Reading waters the mind so that knowledge, imagination, creativity, and sensitivities may grow.

44

MAIL A CARD OR
LETTER TO SOMEONE.

Words can't describe how good it makes a person feel to receive something other than bills in the mail.

Opening a card or letter from you will make the recipient's heart smile.

You can buy a card for ninety-nine cents at Dollar Tree.

Penning a sincere short note will take just a few moments of your time while creating long-lasting joy for the recipient.

45

REALIZE YOUR PURPOSE. ASAP. THEN WALK IN IT.

Mark Twain famously said, "The two most important days of your life are the one you are born and the one you discover why."

We were not created to simply exist.

The Walking Dead is not just a popular television show; those who aimlessly endure each day without purpose or direction are the real *walking dead.*

Realizing your God-designed purpose liberates you from wasting time, energy, and money on things that don't support your life purpose.

"For I know the plans I have for you", declares the Lord, "plans to prosper you and not to harm you, plans to give you a hope and a future." (Jeremiah 29:11)

46

LOSS HAPPENS TO ALL OF US.

Wealth, education, popularity, skill, talent, and even righteous living will not prevent us from experiencing the loss of a loved one.

You may feel as though you're alone, but you aren't. Take as much comfort in that fact as possible.

There is no depth of pain or loss to which God can't descend and bring you from. You are never in a place where God is not.

> The Lord is close to the brokenhearted and saves those who are crushed in spirit. (Psalm 34:18)

47

CELEBRATE OTHERS.

In my experience, the best people seek and celebrate the best *in* other people.

It takes nothing away from you to praise, compliment, promote, and uplift others.

Actually, the extent to which you can celebrate others speaks to your level of maturity and self-actualization.

48

BE GRATEFUL. ALWAYS.

Grateful + Attitude = Gratitude

Being humbly and genuinely thankful for all that you have is more than a disposition; it is a way of life. Gratitude is the way to have the very best life possible. We tend to treasure things that are valuable. When we consider our health and bodies, family and friends, and jobs and resources as gifts rather than entitlements, we care for them by doing all we can to keep them in as healthy a condition as possible.

49

EVERYTHING IS TEMPORARY.

Good times. Bad times. Feelings. Fights. Friendships.
Rainy days. Good meals. Bad smells. Expensive cars.
Aches and pains. Nothing lasts forever.

Accept and embrace what is, while it is, until it isn't.

THE SERENITY PRAYER
God, grant me the serenity to accept
the things I cannot change,
The courage to change the things I can,
And the wisdom to know the difference.

50

EVERYBODY HAS TO GO. THE DEATH RATE IS 100 PERCENT.

All of us are about three generations from being completely unknown (personally, not through books or videos). Don't believe me? Consider how much you recall about time spent with your grandmother's grandmother. Or even your grandmother's mother.

Your children may never know or remember *your* grandparents. The same will be true of you too one day. It's creepy to consider but true nonetheless.

Musicians, movie stars, moguls, ministers, presidents, paupers, and peasants all meet the same fate.

With the fleeting time we have on this earth, we must intentionally live GOLDEN.

Grateful
Optimistic
Loving
Driven
Encouraging (of self and others)
No matter what

All share a common destiny—the righteous and the wicked, the good and the bad, the clean and the unclean, those who offer sacrifices and those who do not. As it is with the good, so with the sinful; as it is with those who take oaths, so with those who are afraid to take them.

This is the evil in everything that happens under the sun: The same destiny overtakes all. The hearts of people, moreover, are full of evil and there is madness in their hearts while they live, and afterward they join the dead.

Anyone who is among the living has hope— even a live dog is better off than a dead lion!

For the living know that they will die, but the dead know nothing; they have no further reward, and even their name is forgotten.

Their love, their hate and their jealousy have long since vanished; never again will they have a part in anything that happens under the sun.

Go, eat your food with gladness, and drink your wine with a joyful heart, for God has already approved what you do.

Always be clothed in white, and always anoint your head with oil. Enjoy life with your wife, whom you love, all the days of this meaningless life that Goad has given you under the sun—all your meaningless days. For this is your lot in life and in your toilsome labor under the sun.

Whatever your hand finds to do, do it with all your might, for in the realm of the dead, where you are going, there is neither working nor planning nor knowledge nor wisdom.

I have seen something else under the sun: The race is not to the swift or the battle to the strong, nor does food come to the wise or wealth to the brilliant or favor to the learned; but time and chance happen to them all.

Moreover, no one knows when their hour will come. (Ecclesiastes 9:2–12)

ABOUT THE AUTHOR

Dionne has been an avid reader and writer since grade school. She has two published novels, GOLDEN CHOICES, and its sequel, GOLDEN LIVES. Dionne and her husband David reside in NE Ohio, and are the parents of three adult children and 2 grand-children.

ACKNOWLEDGEMENT

Thank you for choosing to read this little booklet. The original goal for this book was to encourage and inspire the reader.

Shortly after this project went to publishing, I came under attack in my body, my career, and my family. This book was used to encourage and inspire the author.

BODY ATTACK: Seemingly out-of-the- blue, my lower back completely spasmed and I was totally immobilized. The pain was swift, sharp, and sudden. My focus was soon turned from my back, to my right leg, where constant shooting pains, numbness, and tingling redirected my attention. I was advised that my L4 and L5 were rubbing together. There was no remaining "cushion" between those vertebrae. Not only that, the openings in the vertebrae through which the nerves travel were narrowing. I had tons of questions. Since this condition was degenerative, why was the pain so sudden? And speaking of pain, how could I be rid of it? Why was this happening to me, a person who lives a more-than-moderately healthy lifestyle? How in the world would I ever adjust not wearing high heels?

CAREER ATTACK: There is a big difference between a boss and a leader. It has been said that people don't leave bad jobs, they leave bad management. As Forrest Gump said, "that's all I have to say about that."

FAMILY ATTACK: Ain't no mess like family mess. 'Nuff said.

My life certainly did not mirror Job's, but he seemed more relatable than ever. These types of attacks are not unique to me. Multitudes of people deal with similar, and sadly, far worse situations.

Crazy as it sounds, I have come to be grateful for each and every attack. Enduring these storms have resulted in maturation and increased gratitude beyond imagination.

My appreciation for my family and loved ones is only surpassed by my gratitude for my Lord and Savior, Father and Friend, Creator and Counselor.

My appreciation for you, dear reader, is profound. Despite all you may be experiencing, you have taken the time to read this book.

Life is far from perfect, but thankfully, we can adopt attitudes that allow us to, despite any attack or situation, live GOLDEN.

> **G**rateful
> **O**ptimistic
> **L**oving
> **D**riven
> **E**ncouraging
> **N**o matter what

Printed in the United States
By Bookmasters